BORN TO TASTE
THE GRAPES

by

MIKE MURDOCK

Unless otherwise indicated, all Scripture quotations are taken from the King James Version of the Bible.

Born To Taste The Grapes
Wisdom Key Books
ISBN 1-56394-034-5
Copyright © 1995 by *MIKE MURDOCK*
All publishing rights belong exclusively to Wisdom International

Published by The Wisdom Center
P. O. Box 99 · Denton, Texas 76202
1-888-WISDOM-1 (1-888-947-3661)
Website: www.thewisdomcenter.cc

Why I Wrote This Book.

━━━━━━►≫•◙•≪◄━━━━━━

Man Is A Born Conqueror.

Slavery is unnatural. Our mind functions from the view of the predator, not the prey. We are built to *dominate* the works of God's hands. Thus, the lion and elephant are in the cage, and man became their keeper.

"And God blessed them, and God said unto them, Be fruitful, and multiply, and replenish the earth, and subdue it: and have dominion over the fish of the sea, and over the fowl of the air, and over every living thing that moveth upon the earth" (Gen. 1:28).

Man searches for his greatness.

You possess an obsession to expand, grow and improve. You were born for the "high place." You instinctively gravitate toward increase: spiritually, mentally and financially.

The "Seed of Need" was planted by the Creator. God made Himself a necessity for human happiness. Like the missing puzzle piece, the life picture does not make sense until He is included. We were built for connection. The ear demands sounds, the eye demands sights, the mind wants negotiation, the heart seeks companionship.

The God connection is the bridge from failure to success.

You were born for the *High Places*.

You were born to be *Celebrated*.

You were born to taste *the Grapes of Greatness*.

Never forget it.

That's why I wrote this book.

-*MIKE MURDOCK*

RECOMMENDED BOOKS AND TAPES:
Born To Taste The Grapes (BTS-65/$30 Six-tape series)
The Grasshopper Complex (TS-3/$30 Six-tape series)

◈ 1 ◈

SUCCESS IS JOY.

Success Is Happiness.
Popularity is not success.
Popularity is people liking you.
Happiness is you liking you.

Happiness is feeling good about yourself. It is not necessarily fame, money or position. It is knowledge and awareness of your worth in the eyes of God.

You are here on purpose, designed and equipped for a particular function. You must discern and develop the God-given abilities He invested at your birth. It is only when those gifts are being used properly that you will feel and know the value God sees in you.

Success is *beginning* your Assignment.

Success is *pursuing* your Assignment.

Success is *completing* your Assignment.

Success Is An Instruction Away.

God Never Consults
Your Past
To Determine
Your Future.

-MIKE MURDOCK

2

YOU SHOULD EXPECT ELEVEN BENEFITS FROM GOD.

You Matter To God.

The Book of Ephesians tells us the respect and tenderness in which God views us as His children.

1. *He Has Blessed You.* "Blessed be the God and Father of our Lord Jesus Christ, Who hath blessed us with all spiritual blessings in Heavenly places in Christ" (Eph. 1:3).

2. *He Has Chosen You.* "According as He hath chosen us in Him before the foundation of the world, that we should be holy and without blame before Him in love" (Eph. 1:4).

3. *He Has Predestined You.* "Having predestinated us unto the adoption of children by Jesus Christ to Himself, according to the good pleasure of His will" (Eph. 1:5).

4. *He Has Accepted You.* "To the praise of the glory of His grace,

wherein He hath made us accepted in the beloved" (Eph. 1:6).

5. *He Has Redeemed You.* "In Whom we have redemption through His blood, the forgiveness of sins, according to the riches of His grace" (Eph. 1:7).

6. *He Has Forgiven You.* "In Whom we have redemption through His blood, the forgiveness of sins, according to the riches of His grace" (Eph. 1:7).

7. *He Has Abounded Toward You In Wisdom.* "Wherein He hath abounded toward us in all Wisdom and prudence" (Eph. 1:8).

8. *He Has Made Known To You The Mystery Of His Will.* "Having made known unto us the mystery of His will, according to His good pleasure which He hath purposed in Himself" (Eph. 1:9).

9. *He Has Sealed You.* "In Whom ye also trusted, after that ye heard the word of truth, the gospel of your salvation: in Whom also after that ye believed, ye were sealed with that Holy Spirit of promise" (Eph. 1:13).

10. *He Has Enlightened Your Understanding.* "The eyes of your understanding being enlightened; that ye may know what is the hope of His calling, and what the riches of the glory of His inheritance in the saints" (Eph. 1:18).

11. *He Has Raised You To Sit In Heavenly Places.* "And hath raised us up together, and made us sit together in Heavenly places in Christ Jesus" (Eph. 2:6).

Moses was a winner. He left us two fascinating verses in Deuteronomy 32:13,14 as he described God's dealing with His people in bringing them into greatness:

"He made him ride on the high places of the earth, that he might eat the increase of the fields; and He made him to suck honey out of the rock, and oil out of the flinty rock;...and thou didst drink the pure blood of the grape" (Deut. 32:13,14).

Picture this in your mind:

"...drink the pure blood of the grape."

You and I were born to taste the *Grapes of Blessing.* While some spend their lifetime discussing the size of their giants and problems, other winners dare to reach up for the grapes God promised.

RECOMMENDED BOOKS:
The God Book (B-26/$10)
The Jesus Book (B-27/$10)
The Holy Spirit Handbook (B-100/$10)

☙ **3** ☙

THE GRAPES OF BLESSING REQUIRE YOUR PERSONAL PURSUIT.

⟫▪◦◦⟪

Something Incredible Is Close to You.

God has provided Grapes for you...taste them.

There are two important principles in tasting the grapes of God:

1. *The Grapes Are Not For The Holy, They Are For The Hungry.* Many people feel like they are not good enough to receive the benefits of God. But remember, "They that be whole need not a physician" (Matt. 9:12). The Pharisees never experienced the power and the glory of the Jesus relationship. It was the Samaritan woman at the well and Zacchaeus in the tree who were hungry for His touch, His blessing and His presence.

Maybe you have made a lot of

mistakes in your life. Who hasn't? Some are perhaps more obvious! God knows your heart. He knows how desperately you want to start winning in your life. And He wants you to taste the grapes of favor, the grapes of prosperity, the grapes of health even more than you could ever want them!

Stop looking at your *weaknesses.*

Start concentrating on your *strengths.*

Stop looking backward. (You can't go fast looking through the rear-view mirror!)

"Oh, but Mike, you just don't know the mess I am in!" one lady cried.

"You don't drown by falling in the water, you drown by staying there," I replied.

Get up from your situation. Start setting your success in motion.

2. *The Grapes Are Not Placed Within Your Mouth, They Are Placed Within Your Reach.* Nobody wakes up successful and happy. Many people

think, "Well, if God wanted me healthy, I'd be healthy. If God wanted me financially prosperous, I'd be that way. God is in control."

What is God in control of? He controls the laws of this universe. *He does not control our decisions!* Our decisions create and control the majority of our circumstances!

Stop blaming the sovereignty of God for all of your situations. Use the mind and abilities He has given you to create new and better circumstances. Go after the job He created you for. Take care of the body He has given to you.

The grapes exist: *but you must reach for them.*

The Greatest Quality
On Earth Is
The Willingness
To Become.

-MIKE MURDOCK

❦ 4 ❦

YOU MUST RECOGNIZE THE SEVEN GATES TO THE GRAPES.

You Will Never Possess What You Are Unwilling To Pursue.

We are born to taste the grapes, born to enjoy royalty and the blessings and benefits of God.

You have the instinct for improvement. You have a motivation for increase. Something inside you gravitates toward growth. You were created for expansion. God created you that way, and you will never be happy any other way.

I could speak forever about grapes and how beautiful they are, about the blessings of God—of wealth, health, peace, power, success—but unless you know how to get the grapes, it will not do you any good.

1. The Gate Of Obedience. Deuteronomy 28:1 says, "If thou shalt hearken diligently unto the voice of the Lord thy God" which simply means living up to the knowledge you have received. If you are a gallon, live up to gallon knowledge. If you are a pint, live up to pint knowledge. You can move into stages of perfection and maturity as God reveals Himself to you. Abraham is called a friend of God because he obeyed God.

God said, "Abraham, I want you to move from your comfortable situation and go to a new country," and Abraham obeyed God. If God has been talking to you about something, do it. Do not negotiate.

That raises a question. How can we know the Voice of God? It is impossible to describe the voice of God. Oh, I could give you some guidelines, but when it comes to knowing when God is speaking, you have to get attached to Him. I don't have to ask, "I wonder if this lady is my mother." I know her voice. *If you have spent time in the presence of God, you will know His voice.*

If God is drawing you, speaking to you and dealing with you, obey Him. It may even appear to be a step backward. It may be something you do not want to do. But if you will say, "Father, I will do what You ask me;" if you will step through the Gate of Obedience, all of Heaven will open for you. God is standing by the windows of Heaven ready to pull them open and unload an avalanche of blessings, if you will but obey Him. "Bring ye all the tithes into the storehouse, that there may be meat in Mine house, and prove Me now herewith, saith the Lord of hosts, if I will not open you the windows of Heaven, and pour you out a blessing, that there shall not be room enough to receive it" (Mal. 3:10). He said, "If ye abide in Me, and My words abide in you, ye shall ask what ye will, and it shall be done unto you" (Jn. 15:7). Know the power of obedience.

2. The Gate Of Knowledge. God says, "My people are destroyed for lack of knowledge" (Hos. 4:6). What we do not know can destroy us. God wants us to know. Information is God's business. All of Heaven is involved in distributing information. Angels bring information. The Bible is an information manual. It is literally the "Winner's Digest," informing us about God—His power, nature and thoughts about us—and about angels, satan and demon spirits.

You have a right to the blessings of God. You are a child of the Most High God, an heir of God, a joint-heir with Jesus; He is your elder brother. You do have a right to enter into the Holy of Holies. You do have a High Priest, an Intercessor Who stands beside the right hand of the throne of God on your behalf. But you cannot take hold of the grace and blessings of God unless you have knowledge of what He has provided for you. I am saying that you have to know what belongs to you; you must open and walk through the Gate of Knowledge.

"But without faith it is impossible to please Him: for he that cometh to God must believe that He is, and that He is a rewarder of them that diligently seek Him" (Heb. 11:6).

A woman came forward for prayer one night, and I asked her, "Do you *want* God to heal you?"

"Well," she responded, "I think He is trying to *show me something*."

Have you ever heard of "Disease University?" Many people have accepted disease and sickness as teachers. The Bible says that the Holy Spirit will lead you into all truth. Not, "Yea, I will send disease and it will teach you and lead you into all truth." Know what the Word of God says, and believe it. Pray, "God, your Word says that You were wounded for my transgressions, bruised for my iniquities and by Your stripes I am healed" (read Isa. 53:5). Claim the Word and stand upon it. You can spend your energy explaining your sickness, or you can spend your energy *reaching for a miracle.*

Do you have knowledge of the grapes God has provided? Find out what the Scriptures teach; know about the grapes you are reaching for. You were born to taste the grapes, and you need to have the knowledge that God did make them available and accessible to you. A lot of people do not receive because they do not even know the grapes exist.

3. The Gate Of Visualization.

Visualize the grapes. If you cannot see the grapes in your mind, you will not see them in time. Your mind is a force that affects everything else in your life. The renewing of your mind is the secret of transformation. "I beseech you therefore, brethren, by the mercies of God, that ye present your bodies a living sacrifice, holy, acceptable unto God, which is your reasonable service. And be not conformed to this world: but be ye transformed by the renewing of your mind, that ye may prove what is that good, and acceptable, and perfect, will of God" (Rom. 12:1,2). Your mind is a powerful force.

The woman with the issue of blood said to herself, "If I may touch but His clothes, I shall be whole" (Mk. 5:28). She visualized. It happened in her body. Visualize the grapes; see yourself tasting the grapes. See yourself with victory. Some of us have never seen ourselves victorious like God means for us to see ourselves.

Visualize where God wants you to be, and then act as if you are *already there.*

Jesus visualized Himself in victory: "...for the joy that was set before Him [He] endured the cross" (Heb. 12:2). He endured the present suffering for the joy that was set before Him; His mind was picturing victory. When Jesus walked to Calvary, He was not looking at the cross; He was looking at the resurrection.

If you have always longed to be victorious in an area, get your mind on the grapes until you can visualize them and see them in your grasp. Is there a habit in your life you want to conquer? Do not concentrate on the habit; concentrate on victory. This is called the *Law of Displacement.* It means you displace evil by the entrance of good. We do not go into a building and suggest to darkness, "Would you mind leaving, because if you leave we can have light?" We bring in light, and the entrance of light forces the exit of darkness.

Some people spend their lives saying, "Oh, I wish I could quit thinking bad thoughts." You will

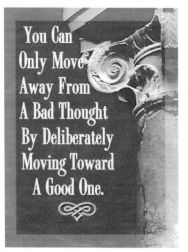

You Can Only Move Away From A Bad Thought By Deliberately Moving Toward A Good One.

never stop thinking bad thoughts, you will never stop thinking doubt until you start thinking faith and you start seeing yourself victorious. That picture drives out evil. Visualize it right now. Whatever it is, see yourself with it.

4.   The Gate Of Forgiveness. The fourth gate to the grapes is *forgiveness, which simply means the transferral of the right to judge and penalize.* It means that you give up your position on God's vengeance team. Forgiveness does not flow to you until it can flow through you. You can ask for forgiveness, beg God for forgiveness, offer Him "double tithe," but nothing will happen inside you until you permit God alone to penalize somebody for doing you wrong.

"Well, Mike, I want to teach him a lesson."

That's understandable, but it is wrong. God is the One in charge of payment; He is the Judge. Exercise the ability to withhold judgment, and let God perform His program of restoration and forgiveness.

Forgiveness is the removal of information and the pain of it. There is no entry into Heaven until we walk through the Gate of Forgiveness. There are no grapes of blessing, no grapes of reward, until we "remember...not the former things" (Isa. 43:18).

Forgive not only other people, but forgive yourself. That is just as important. There are people who have never forgiven themselves. Do not advertise your mistakes. Lay the memory of them at the Cross and leave it there. Jesus is your sacrifice!

5. The Gate Of Persistence. What is the Gate of Persistence? Simply make up your mind, regardless of how far away the grapes appear, to push on for the blessing. Sometimes it will seem like they are a thousand miles away. Friends may try to discourage and disillusion you. They may not understand your dream, your goal. It will not fall into your lap. It will not be easy. But every man or woman who has ever achieved anything had to persist. They made up their mind to go after what they believed in.

I met a young man the other day —sharp, nice, could be a great preacher. Will he ever be? I doubt it. Why? No persistence: "Well, I tried and it didn't work, I think I will quit. I don't know if I am called."

The power belongs to the persistent. For ten days the disciples waited in the upper room. Can you imagine the first day? Someone says, "Well, he said for us to just wait; here we are." Second day, third, fourth, fifth, sixth. Another says, "You know, if God really wanted us to have power, He wouldn't make us just sit here and wait for it." Seventh day. Eighth. Ninth. Tenth—suddenly, a sound from Heaven as a rushing mighty wind fills the room (see Acts 2:2). Cloven tongues of fire sit upon their heads, and they begin to speak in tongues as the Spirit of God gives them utterance. Why? Persistence.

Say it: Persistence. Say it until your whole body feels it. There will be times you will not feel like you can make it. At times you will feel like asking, "Why am I doing this anyway?" Or you will feel like it's no use, nothing is going to work out. Stay there! The diseased woman didn't feel like pushing her way through the crowd, but she had a goal. I am certain Peter did not always feel like a big overcomer, but God gave him such a victory that when he, the man who had denied the Lord, began to preach, he said, "You people need to repent; you denied the Holy One of Israel." "Him, being delivered by the determinate counsel and fore-knowledge of God, ye have taken, and by wicked hands have crucified and slain" (Acts 2:23). He persisted until the power of God came into his life, and he walked in that power.

6. The Gate Of Sowing. You cannot reap grapes until you *sow* grapes. The Blessing follows the

Blesser. *Whatever good thing I do for another, God is going to do for me.* "Knowing that whatsoever good thing any man doeth, the same shall he receive of the Lord, whether he be bond or free" (Eph. 6:8). If I want to taste grapes, I have to distribute grapes. I have to bless other people, if I want God to bless me.

If I want something good to happen in my life, I must make something good happen for my sister or brother. I must first perform for others what God wants to perform for me.

Jesus did not say that if you treat your brother or sister right, he or she will love you. He said that if you do right to others, God will do right by you. Everything reproduces after its own kind. If you want healing, start praying for others to experience healing. If you want blessing, start concentrating on others receiving blessing. Jesus concentrated on other people's needs. He went around doing good, healing all that were sick and oppressed by the devil. "How God anointed Jesus of Nazareth with the

Holy Ghost and with power: Who went about doing good, and healing all that were oppressed of the devil; for God was with Him" (Acts 10:38).

What You Make Happen For Others, God Will Make Happen For You.

7. The Gate Of Praise. Judah, which means praise, was the first tribe into battle. Praise is the sound that makes hell sick; it unnerves demons. Satan used to be the song leader in Heaven, but God kicked him out. Anytime you start praising God, all of Heaven notices it. Let the redeemed of the Lord say so; make a joyful noise; clap your hands.

Praise is an act of the will. It is not something you have to feel in order for it to be real. It is not meditation; it is something that is heard. Praise is articulated sound and opinion. It is your recognition of Jesus as Lord of everything, that Jehovah is still on the throne.

When we begin to praise God, something happens. I do not care how you feel; if you start saying, "God, I love you," something loosens. Talk about smashing the locks of your prison; praise does that! Now, praise has nothing to do with feelings. You do not have to say, "God, I feel great," or, "I feel lousy." Praise has to do with Him, and it takes your mind off yourself. Praise lifts you to where God is.

God is very comfortable with praise. In fact, that is where He chooses to dwell. "But Thou art holy, O Thou that inhabitest the praises of Israel" (Ps. 22:3). God likes praise, and He responds to it. Not only does God respond to praise, demons react to it.

Praise is something you deliberately choose to do, to acknowledge the power of God. Say, "I love You, Jesus. You are wonderful, Jesus." The purpose of praise is not just to make us feel good, but it is also so other people will hear. God enjoys advertisement! He does things in a big way. You never see God sneaking around saying, "You be quiet now and have a good time." He is a celebration God, an expressive God.

You were born to taste the grapes

of God's blessing. The silver and gold are His. He gives us the power to get wealth. Everything that God has, everything that He is, He is willing to pour into us and through us. The grapes are not for the holy, they are for the hungry. They are not placed within your mouth; they are placed within your reach.

Enter the gates and reach for the grapes.

Only Pursuers Qualify.

Our prayer together...

"Holy Spirit, You are the Giver of all the Grapes of Blessing. Teach me how to receive them and use me to bless others around me. In Jesus' name. Amen."

You Can Have It.

- ▶ Why Sickness Is Not The Will Of God
- ▶ How To Release The Powerful Forces That Guarantee Blessing
- ▶ The Incredible Role Of Your Memory And The Imagination
- ▶ The Hidden Power Of Imagination And How To Use It Properly
- ▶ The Difference Between The Love Of God And His Blessings
- ▶ 3 Steps In Increasing Your Faith
- ▶ 2 Rewards That Come When You Use Your Faith In God
- ▶ 7 Powerful Keys Concerning Your Faith

Dreams and desires begin as photographs within our hearts and minds – things that we want to happen in our future. God plants these pictures as invisible Seeds within us. God begins every miracle in your life with a seed-picture... the invisible idea that gives birth to a visible blessing. In this teaching, you will discover your desires and how to concentrate on watering and nurturing the growth of your Dream-Seeds until you attain your God-given goals.

Your Letter Is Very Important To Me

You are a special person to me, and I believe that you are special to God. I want to assist you in any way possible. Write me when you need an intercessor to pray for you. When you write, my staff and I will pray over your letter. I will write you back.

Mike, please enter into the prayer of agreement
with me for the following needs:
(Please Print)

_____

_____

_____

_____

_____

_____

_____

_____

_____

_____

_____

_____

Clip and Mail

Mail To:
The Wisdom Center · P.O. Box 99 · Denton, Texas 76202
1-888-WISDOM-1 (1-888-947-3661)
Website: www.thewisdomcenter.cc

DECISION

Will You Accept Jesus As Your Personal Savior Today?

The Bible says, "That if thou shalt confess with thy mouth the Lord Jesus, and shalt believe in thine heart that God hath raised Him from the dead, thou shalt be saved" (Rom. 10:9).

Pray this prayer from your heart today!

"Dear Jesus, I believe that you died for me and rose again on the third day. I confess I am a sinner...I need Your love and forgiveness...Come into my heart. Forgive my sins. I receive Your eternal life. Confirm Your love by giving me peace, joy and supernatural love for others. Amen."

DR. MIKE MURDOCK

is in tremendous demand as one of the most dynamic speakers in America today.

More than 14,000 audiences in 38 countries have attended his meetings and seminars. Hundreds of invitations come to him from churches, colleges, and business corporations. He is a noted author of over 130 books, including the best sellers, *"The Leadership Secrets of Jesus"* and *"Secrets of the Richest Man Who Ever Lived."* Thousands view his weekly television program, *"Wisdom Keys with Mike Murdock."* Many attend his Saturday School of Wisdom Breakfasts that he hosts in major cities in America.

❑ Yes, Mike! I made a decision to accept Christ as my personal Savior today. Please send me my free gift of your book *"31 Keys to a New Beginning"* to help me with my new life in Christ. *(B-48)*

Name_____ Birth date ___/___

Address_____

City_____ State_____ Zip_____

Phone (____)_____ E-Mail_____

Mail To:

B-65

The Wisdom Center · P.O. Box 99 · Denton, TX 76202
1-888-WISDOM-1 (1-888-947-3661)
Website: www.thewisdomcenter.cc